my cool caravan.

my cool caravan.

an inspirational guide to retro-style caravans

jane field-lewis + chris haddon

photography by **hilary walker**

contents

introduction – how it all began

Looking for somewhere to spend inexpensive weekends away, or a place to work, or for a child to play, or even a little private hideaway? The humble caravan ticks all of these boxes.

Chris, my co-author, and I both store our caravans at a farm in Sussex, and it was whilst there, reflecting on the joys of retro caravans, and the re-discovery of simple pleasures, we realised we shared this same passion. That is how the idea for this book came about.

My Cool Caravan is by no means a comprehensive guide, but it is our way of celebrating the delights of the vintage caravan.

We have enjoyed many conversations with caravan owners who have shared happy childhood memories with us – exciting trips to foreign countries, holidays in English seaside towns and evenings spent listening to dad's jazz records with the rain pattering on the roof. Happy memories of simple things, reflecting the valuable details of life which are usually too readily overlooked.

Caravans give us the opportunity to appreciate these details. To take time out and enjoy life in the slow lane... to notice the early morning mist on a lake, the character of a duck's quack, the lovely low evening light and the peace and quiet   all simple things so easily missed in our jam-packed busy lives. A caravan gives us the chance to enjoy these uncomplicated pleasures without suffering too much.

There have always been some stalwarts who have recognized, preserved and restored early models; people who realised that they were buying into a little piece of social and design history. Whilst researching this book we have come across a number of these early visionaries who have been happy to allow us to photograph their labours of love and share their stories with us. We are grateful to those who had the vision and the belief in these projects and several of their caravans are featured here.

This book aims to explore the hidden world of creativity and design afforded by the humble caravan. Apart from the historically important examples, the proliferation of mass-produced models from the 1960s onwards opens up so many possibilities. You can be creative, indulge your sense of nostalgia, restore something to its former glory, or design a modern version of the original style. Or you can do something totally new.

The days of utilitarian tin mugs and chipped crockery are a thing of the past. Nowadays it's easy to make your caravan look attractive with a few simple touches – a pretty coffee pot, goose-down duvets and comfortable pillows. Arm yourself with a collection of old novels that you've always intended to read or a drawing book and coloured pencils, maybe some old board games from the charity shop – all means of creating those valuable memories and having time to do something a world away from your everyday life.

We are both relatively new to caravanning, so our first purchases were broached with caution. Mine was a tiny, orange and brown 1970s-style caravan that has since been modestly re-dressed with a sunshade, curtains stitched from second-hand fabric, and cupboards filled with vintage Tupperware and cast-off family china from my teenage years. It's been a joy to add to it over time and the cost has been minimal. It's a continued pleasure to spot new treasures found in vintage stores or on the internet.

Chris truly has the bug – he now owns three caravans. One has been converted into a home studio from which he runs his business; he leaves the second one in the countryside for family holidays and uses the third as a movable weekend getaway. We have both come to acknowledge that there are a growing number of people like us, who recognize the inherent design possibilities and are drawn to taking on these delightful little projects. We hope that they will inspire and interest you too.

Many people are already well into this trend. Music festivals are testaments to many a groovy caravanner and the plethora of online blogs reveal a world of retro-inspired caravans with cute interiors, where young people are running small businesses from cup cakes to art galleries to tattoo parlours. Similarly, the generation of VW camper owners, who love the idea of getting up and going but find they need a bit more space and flexibility, and the people who have grown up with the concept of the boutique hotel, can now have their own old or new customized version on wheels, complete with wi-fi and designer furnishings.

This book would not have been possible without the enthusiastic endorsement of other caravan owners who have shared their journeys with us. We are indebted to the collectors and historians of caravanning, to those who have written the books, collected the china, cherished the old family photographs and spent time researching original parts and fittings – all with a great sense of pride.

We hope that the photographs and stories in this book will inspire you to embark on your own project. It doesn't require huge sums of money and provides the opportunity to enjoy a simpler space, and to embrace the many possibilities of the humble caravan.

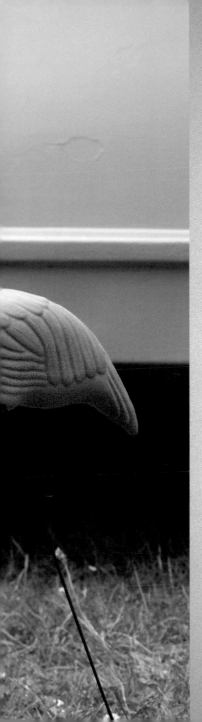

new retro

For us, new retro represents the modern version of traditional homeliness and family life. Vintage objects, bunting, retro china, rose prints and a multitude of colour – things reminiscent of happy childhood memories – can become part of the decor and can often be found in a charity shop or a car boot sale.

The creation of that 'comfortable' look, but with strong contemporary overtones, is a nostalgic look back to earlier times, when most owners were aiming to create a happy family space.

The look works well with caravans pre-dating the 1960s, particularly those from the 1950s. From the Cheltenham Springbok with its homely curves, to 'Constance', the Sprite 14 – one of the early models from Sam Alpers 'Sprite' corporation and the forerunner of the best-selling Sprite Musketeer – the overriding look and feeling is modern, but evocative of a time gone by.

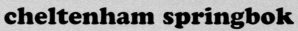
cheltenham springbok

Lydia, the proud owner of this rare Cheltenham caravan explains: 'We were looking for the perfect retreat, and at first we purchased a beach hut in Minehead. Although it was lovely, it wasn't mobile so we tried narrow boating. Again, we had great fun but found it too restrictive, we needed more freedom. A caravan seemed the next obvious port of call, so we bought a small Cheltenham Fawn and from then on we were hooked!'

Lydia and her husband quickly outgrew the Fawn and upgraded to a modern, retro-style caravan for more space. They took a few trips in it but felt it lacked the charm of an older caravan. After a lot of searching they found this Cheltenham Springbok, one of only a few still in existence.

'After a lot of trial and error we have now finally found the right form of escape and have never looked back.'

style notes

A relaxed palette of warm-toned colours is used to create a family-friendly, contemporary space. The inclusion of a traditional rose design on fabric and hand-towels, a re-issued Roberts radio and family games, reinforces the updated classic English theme.

Textiles are a complementary mix of floral, checked and striped. The mix works by keeping the scale of print consistent and using red as the harmonising colour.

The floral fabric used on the upholstery is a Cath Kidston print, and traditional linoleum checkerboard tiling has been used for the floor. The traditional lantern roof provides a soft top-light and the windows are simply dressed with striped cotton curtains and tie backs.

beegle bus vw

This beautiful Beegle bus is a 1971 Volkswagen camper-van imported from California and owned by Bella Clark, daughter-in-law of the iconic textile designer Celia Birtwell and legendary fashion designer Ossie Clark.

Bella was bitten by the VW bug at an early age: 'My father had a 1971 VW Danbury, so when I spotted this one for sale I needed no persuading. She was in fantastic condition when we purchased her... We were lucky, the previous owner had done a lot of the hard work,' comments Bella.

'After weighing up the pros and cons we installed a TV in place of the sink... this was partly due to the unpredictability of the British weather and three young children! Now we love going off camping for the weekend, whenever we want to and whatever the weather.'

style notes

Personal touches were added to this classic VW by making curtains, cushions and bunting from Celia Birtwell fabric. Using folding chairs and tables also in Birtwell fabric means that the style is continued both inside and out, a particularly useful device when dressing a small space.

Items that roll, fold flat or stack are essential when transporting furniture and ensuring that they look good, whether in use or put away adds to the visual pleasure of a small space.

Another example of Bella's attention to scale is the use of half-size bunting around the windows – the effect is the same but it is not overpowering.

constance

At the end of Lucy and Steve's garden, hidden by trees, sits a little sanctuary: 'Our daughter Phoebe had asked for a playhouse for her birthday to replace her tired, dejected one,' explains Lucy. 'A caravan seemed like a good idea, more resilient against the weather and fun too. Not only that, it was cheaper and bigger than a replacement shed and came fully equipped!'

Lucy and Steve found 'Constance' (the birthday girl's middle name) on an internet auction site: 'She arrived in a good, clean condition. We just needed to "pretty" her up.'

In fact, the whole family seems to have found a use for Constance: 'Phoebe and her friends spend many happy hours in there playing while Rosie, our teenage daughter, goes to Constance to escape from things, mainly her parents! Even we like to go and sit in there sometimes, for a quiet coffee and to savour the peacefulness and watch the wildlife.'

style notes

The owner's eye for style has created another modern take on a period caravan. The exterior has been re-sprayed in a gorgeous 'Brighton Seafront' green, which perfectly reflects its 1950s heritage.

The traditional linoleum flooring and seats covered in wipe-clean vinyl are both in keeping with the '50s mood. Given that this is primarily a playhouse, the styling is also a practical solution – nothing becomes too precious – and a happy mixture of retro-styled cushions and blankets help to offset the hard surfaces and add visual interest. Refurbishing the interior with classic British childhood items – the handmade crochet rug, vintage picnic set, melamine cups and hand-knit toys – have created a happy space. It is a look that appeals to children and adults alike.

amphibious caravan

The present owners of this extraordinary Trail-It amphibious caravan are at a bit of a loss to know what to do with it, as it was purchased mainly for its rarity and individuality.

Believed to have been built in 1965, this caravan boat has retractable wheels and a removable 'A-frame' but its huge weight makes it too cumbersome for the narrow British roads; for now it looks like this little dreamboat will have to get to its destinations by water only.

It was designed and built in the USA and although similar British versions were developed, they never really achieved high sales. However, in recent times there seems to have been a slight resurgence in interest and the combination of a caravan and boat could well become something more desirable in years to come.

style notes

The fresh-looking, white interior of this intriguing dual-purpose caravan/boat is enhanced by a scrubbed wooden floor. Each item has been carefully chosen so the interior keeps its uncluttered, simple design

Basic enamel saucepans, an old aluminium coffee pot and plain white curtains are both economical and stylish. It is not necessary to spend large sums of money to achieve this look; keep clutter to a minimum, avoid loud patterns and let each object speak for itself.

diddy

'Luckily for us, the sellers neglected to put a reserve price on Diddy, the caravan, when we found her for sale on the internet, so we snapped her up for £150', explains Emma. 'The caravan was in a sorry state when we collected her. She had been used by the previous owners as a mobile dog kennel when taking their beloved dogs to shows. After a lot of cleaning and dog hair removal we gave her a new lease of life in a "sympathetic" retro style.'

Despite the caravan's small size (it's only 10-foot long, hence its nickname), the whole family manage to spend plenty of weekends away in it.

'It's a bit of a squeeze inside,' admits Emma, 'and we do get a few looks of disbelief when my partner and I, our two children and the dog step out in the morning! There's no room for a TV, but we really don't miss it.'

style notes

Refurbished with maximum style and minimum spend, Diddy's quirky original features have been left well alone.

Shabby, but well-loved stuffed toys find a happy home among re-used picnic hampers, vintage horticultural wooden boxes, a charming mix of odd napkins and tea towels and cutlery in a variety of styles. Cushions always look best when they are not identical shapes or sizes. Here vintage Scandinavian fabric has been used alongside a modern 'Amy Butler' print to striking effect. It's always best to strive for a happy coincidence rather than an over-considered, co-ordinated affair.

The cheerful vintage travel stickers on the rear window are beautifully English and a reminder of Diddy's younger days and travels, as is the old deckchair strapped to the luggage rack. Such features are always good to leave in place.

country cottage

Many people love the idea of owning a country cottage.

There is something about the innate prettiness, the cosy comfortable surroundings, leaded light windows, English roses and afternoon tea that have an enduring appeal. In reality, this idyll can be achieved through your choice of caravan and its interior decoration.

The caravans in this section range from the very early 1936 Eccles Aristocrat, a popular quality brand designed to appeal to the middle-class caravanning market, to the Winchester Pipet, designed by Bertram Hutchings, an influential early caravan designer and founder of the Winchester brand. Both caravans have a characteristic, curved lantern roof with leaded skylights, oak cabinets and classic linoleum flooring. Top-quality fittings and comfort were valued by the relatively affluent purchasers of the time, who were also the first generation to acquire cars that could potentially tow a caravan.

The design of these caravans echoed the styles of the day. Eccles were supplied with an Art Deco sunburst-style gas fire, ceramic sink and drainer and a built in radio with a classic geometric grille design. With this level of comfort, sturdiness and sense of space you could almost forget that you were in a caravan.

The country cottage style is still popular today, and although the exterior of a caravan may not reflect this, the interior decor will clearly illustrate the look.

The Freelander caravan has none of the exterior features of a country cottage style, but is simple and honest looking enough to carry the style internally. Its modern chintz-floral wallpaper, rose-print cushions, delicately painted floral motifs and decorative lighting continues this theme in very modern form.

eccles aristocrat

'My wife and I have been caravanning now for far too many years to mention' says Jim. 'During that time I have owned and restored plenty of different caravans. This particular model is a 1936 Eccles Aristocrat and one of my favourites. Many people think I have re-sprayed it, but, in fact, the blue is the original factory colour.'

Jim and his wife are now accustomed to the amount of head-turning and attention the caravan attracts, thanks in part to their commitment to stay loyal to the original features: 'We have kept the inside as original as possible as we attend quite a few classic caravan rallies and it's just not the "done thing" to tinker too much and change all of its original features. Caravans from all decades have their admirers. I personally lean towards pre-war caravans purely because of the craftsmanship.'

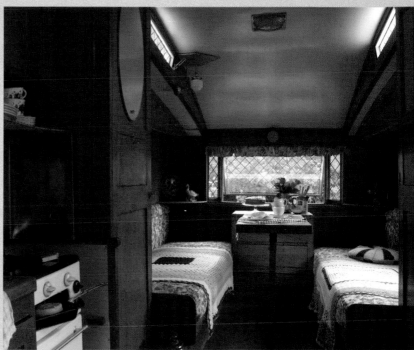

style notes

There is a bit of responsibility involved when you are the owner of an important historical caravan. With only a few models like this one left, they are best looked after carefully and only modernized where absolutely necessary.

Here, many original features have been maintained – the oak cupboards, original cooker, sink and lovely zinc draining board, though the radio is not original. The grille and the surround are original and are classic Art Deco style. The seating has been re-covered but the original pale green fabric has been respectfully retained beneath.

That this delightful caravan, which is more than 70 years old, is still in use and roadworthy is down to its owner respecting the past and finding an appropriate and unobtrusive way to add modern necessities.

ol' 36

'I can confidently claim that 'Ol' 36 is the oldest, most original, full-sized road-registered caravan in Australia,' boasts Bob of New South Wales, Australia.

'She may look like a British caravan but she was actually built in Australia in 1936, using a British chassis and components supplied by Brockhouse Engineering.'

'She was built just after The Great Depression and prior to World War II,' adds Bob, 'but, in reality, she would not have had much use until the mid-1940s. She was actually last registered in 1961. The interior was in very good original condition when we bought her in 2006. We just love her.'

style notes

Ol' 36 comes from between the wars, when many people left the cities to live in the suburbs and the growth in suburban architecture meant that many people adopted a new style of home. The 'streamlined moderne' movement was very forward-looking for its time. It was a branch of Art Deco, with simple lines, beautiful rounded forms and minimal decoration. People wanted lighter, brighter houses and curvy window forms followed. This was also the era of Clarice Cliff ceramics and grand ocean-liner style. Notice the windows – the 'Sunburst' shape was characteristic of the period, as was the subtle, pale colour scheme of the exterior.

winchester pipet

A fascination with caravanning can begin at any time of life, as Peter, owner of this 1954 Winchester Pipet proves. 'We picked up the caravanning bug about six years ago,' he says. 'I've always had a thing for vintage cars and a vintage caravan seemed the obvious accessory. It came into its own when we exhibited our car at shows but now the tables have turned and the caravan has become the main focus. We tend to exhibit the caravan more than the car!'

Peter continues: 'Caravans eventually took on a different appearance and the more box-shaped mass-produced models soon appeared on the market. You could say the classic shape of this Winchester was the end of an era as the shape had been around for more than 25 years prior in many different guises, so it was about time to make way for more modern styling and the new materials of the 1960s.'

style notes

There is something very comfortable and liveable about the interior of this 1954 caravan. It has a relaxed feel, with 1950s' embroidered cushions, vintage caravan books and retro crockery. It is less of a 'roses around the door' type of country cottage caravan, and more about getting back in touch with nature. It is a simple, earnest space that reminds you never to forget what is outside the window.

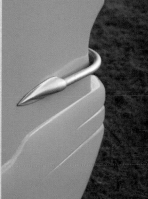

A farm in Ireland is the next destination for this 1950s Freeman caravan. It will be nestled in the corner of an old apple yard to battle against the Atlantic gales – as owner Marika intends to use this quirky little caravan as a retreat for her to write in.

This latest incarnation is one of several notable changes that the caravan has experienced. The previous owner was designer and writer Pearl Lowe, who purchased the caravan with the intention of using it as a 'boudoir' style den at her wedding. She later used the caravan to unwind in and write her memoirs.

'The curvaceous fibreglass exterior was originally intended to be painted gold, but instead it was finished in the mint green colouring that you see today – personally, I think it fits in better with the leafy green countryside where it now resides.'

'I find the interior very calming' comments Marika. 'Despite first appearances nothing within the caravan really demands visual attention, it all tends to harmonise into a very relaxing place.'

freeman

style notes

Two classic wallpapers are used here – Coles' Hummingbirds and Ralph Lauren's re-working of a classic English floral motif. The benefit of wallpapering a caravan is that with only one roll you can instantly change the feel of the space. It is the genteel nature of both wallpaper designs that makes this look work. The clever addition of a chandelier and the painted flower motif and metal sculptured rose complete the boudoir feel and make this country caravan utterly modern and glamorous.

old retro

Mass production of caravans, and hence their increased affordability, peaked in the 1960s and 70s. Manufacturers were quick to develop their brands in a fast-changing and profitable market and as a result brands like Sprite, Abi, and Ci Cadet became both popular and fashionable.

Caravan technology was developing at a pace, too, and as a result the 1970s saw the beginnings of double glazing, better insulation and even built-in fridges – the start of the modern conveniences that we all now take for granted. The shapes of the caravans were modern for their times, too – slightly boxy with rounded edges.

We still see these caravans in their hundreds – on the road, at campsites and at festivals – and there is still a certain charm to features such as plaid upholstery, laminate wood veneer finishes and the combination of oranges and browns used in the colour schemes.

Their interiors are not only suited to the use of modern plastics, but things you may not have previously considered for your caravan – funky fabrics, orange enamel saucepans, Tupperware and the shag pile rug – all happily find new homes and look fabulous!

monza 1000

Stylist and co-author of this book, Jane Field-Lewis was looking for something different – a release from the pressures of her day job – and found it in this 1970s Monza Caravan.

Jane co-owns the Monza with a friend: 'We purchased it just over four years ago for a few hundred pounds... it's been worth many more times that in enjoyment. Towing it isn't our cup of tea, so it happily stays on a farm in Sussex, a little tiny hideaway,' comments Jane.

'Styling something for myself makes a nice change and is particularly fun as decorating decisions can be changed in a moment. My caravan is the perfect place to escape from my busy working life and is where I recharge my creative batteries. As my job involves sourcing items for photo shoots, I come across quirky objects everyday. I used to squirrel these away for future projects, but now I get distracted and buy things to dress the caravan instead.'

'My husband is a fair-weather camper who is now slowly coming around to my way of thinking. My son, on the other hand, needed no convincing and has embraced outdoor living.'

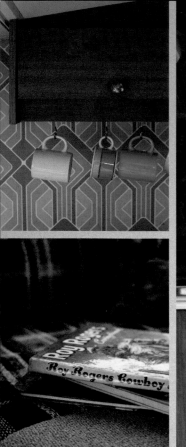

style notes

Colour trends change with time. This is a classic example of 1970s brown. Brown is not always a fashionable colour but the '70s brown was a warm earthy tone and incredibly modern for its time. The exterior of this caravan, its signage, upholstery and formica walls with brown hessian print all feature the colour. Accompanying colours are best kept similarly warm, hence the addition of gold, mustard and custardy yellows to the decor. The '70s vinyl wallpaper came from old unused stock and the crockery – the classic Denby's Midwinter 'Sun' design, once commonplace and now highly collectable – was chosen because it features similar tones.

eriba familia

'We initially got "into" camping when our parents took us as kids,' says Rikki, owner of this extremely rare, four-berth 1967 Eriba Familia. 'More recently for us, it's a great way to escape London. We first had a VW camper van, but as our two daughters, Lulu and Daisy, got older and taller, the camper van was just not big or practical enough.'

Rikki eventually came across this little gem on the internet but despite contacting the seller as soon as he saw it, it had already been sold.

'I wanted the caravan so badly that I asked the seller to contact the guy who had just bought it to ask if he wanted to sell it at a profit. To my amazement the guy said yes! The deal was done and two days later the caravan was in my garage!'

Rikki's fast work and determination meant the family could soon start enjoying the Eriba: 'We tow the caravan with my wife Vivienne's 1962 VW Type 3 Squareback and my 1954 Deluxe Microbus. Both vehicles handle the job with ease, even when the caravan is fully loaded with the family bikes.'

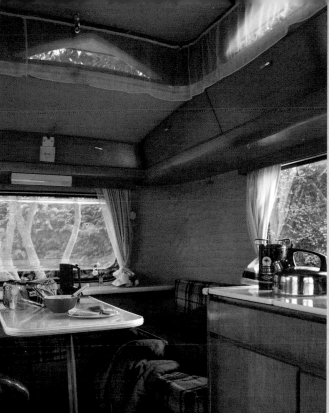
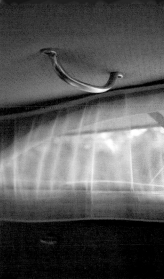
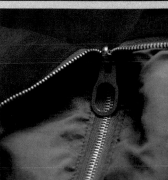

style notes

The relaxed, youthful camping style of this favoured brand of the VW fraternity, is an inexpensive and groovy way to enjoy the outdoors life. The tone is achieved by using retro-styled sleeping bags, feather-stuffed vintage eiderdowns, plastic bowls and Tupperware storage containers. Otherwise, the interior has been left alone, there was no need to change the pop-top, or the upholstery – it's a classic piece of design... just like the VW.

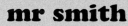

mr smith

This distinctive testament to 1970s retro styling can be found on the owner's property and is an unintentional time warp of interior design, filled with all that the decade had to offer.

Mr Smith's caravan is parked in his own nature garden which he landscaped over 20 years ago. 'The caravan has been in situ for about seven years now,' says Mr Smith. 'It's sometimes used by our guests to spend the night in but is mainly used by the family for quiet time and breathing space whilst enjoying the wildlife and beautiful ponds that are around the grounds.'

'No-one knows the make or exact age. I have looked everywhere on the van itself but there are no clues. It doesn't really matter to us as it's the pleasure that it brings to my whole family that counts.'

style notes

The *raison d'être* of this caravan is its fabulous, hidden location – it is a superb vantage point to watch the birds, enjoy the changing seasons and enjoy the solitude of the natural environment. An old pair of binoculars, a collection of bird books, vintage placemats and tableware and a vase of wild flowers and grasses set the scene inside. The heavily patterned original upholstery has been partially covered with a mixture of old knitted blankets and a goatskin rug – all adding textures and a sense of warmth and comfort. Textured surfaces always work best when the light hits them, preferably from the side, and in this instance the large picture windows face south, over the lake, providing ample sun.

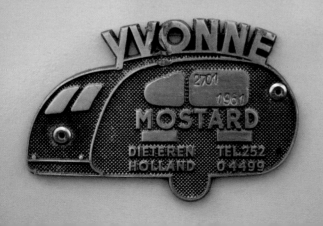

mostard

Dutch manufacturer Mostard started producing caravans around 1959 and continued production until the late 1970s. The caravans are now very collectable, especially in Holland where there are clubs devoted to them.

'I spotted our van in an old outbuilding in Holland, it was completely untouched,' says owner Neil. 'The owner had no intention of getting rid of it but after some persuasion he agreed to sell it to us. That was a year ago. It has since undergone a complete and sympathetic restoration. I have carried out some research and have found out that this could be the very first one of its kind.'

In spite of its status, Neil and Emma continue to enjoy their Mostard, mainly to take the family camping: 'We do get a buzz from knowing that we are among the very few people to have the privilege of owning one of these pieces of caravan history – it's about as retro as you can get really.'

style notes

'There is a place for everything and everything in its place.' This well-used phrase is especially apt when you own a caravan. This Mostard isn't a big space, but it makes use of items that are foldable or stackable and tables with legs that unscrew. Everything needs to be able to be packed away. The Mostard Yvonnes were well regarded for their quality carpentry and had delightful birch ply cupboard doors with aluminium trim, chunky hinges and sturdy metal catches which had a satisfying clunky mechanism. These were all quality details that became partially lost in the mass-produced era that followed.

ci cadet

This caravan was destined for new owners until Suzanne had a change of heart and decided to keep this little treasure to give to her eight-year-old niece. It has only had one owner from new, so its features are original, and the addition of 1970s funky flower vinyl stickers dotted inside and out completes the retro feel.

The caravan sits in the garden surrounded by wild flowers: 'My niece is very protective of her caravan-come-playhouse. She keeps it clean and always ensures that the door is locked at night. I'm so glad we didn't sell the caravan,' admits Suzanne. 'It's not always about the money, instead it's about the enjoyment and memories my niece will take with her through to adulthood.'

style notes

A caravan is a quick and easy way to establish a bit of your own space – this lucky girl has her own playhouse, courtesy of a generous aunt. It is filled with favourite possessions, food playsets, quirky soft toys and books. The contents will no doubt change as she grows older but it will always be a perfect den in which to entertain friends.

Mum sourced some 1970s-style fabric on the internet and has sewn curtains for three of the four windows...there wasn't quite enough so she is still looking for one more piece!

It makes a lovely environment, come rain or shine.

the simple life

Consider a life without any pressures or problems and without the need to work in order to survive. Imagine the authentic travellers' way of life, having time on your hands and no particular place to go. Trying to capture just part of that existence – even for a few days, will put problems into perspective and provide a sense of freedom.

We tend to surround ourselves with the latest luxuries and, let's face it, there are so many products promising to make our lives easier. Do we really need them? We often find ourselves happier when we return to a simpler lifestyle.

In reality the basic necessities of life that we all need in order to survive are still the same – all that has happened is that 'clutter' has got in the way.

Let's take a step back. Look at the interior of a caravan and consider what are the basic requirements. This is the first step in achieving a simpler lifestyle. Then start adding your own design ideas – these could include new or old objects; rustic materials; soft cosy fabrics; exposed wood grain and a sprinkling of personal items. The key is to keep it simple – introduce individuality but not over-complication.

Algy Sloane, the owner of this awe-inspiring, converted horsebox explains, 'I have been slightly obsessed with the UK traveller scene of the 1970s, 1980s and 1990s. Unfortunately, the hedonistic lifestyle was quashed in the late 1990s and for various reasons many beautiful traveller vans ended up impounded or were taken abroad along with their owners. My wife and I bought this horse box in 2003 and slowly and meticulously we have transformed it into a comfy living space.'

'Having used it for our honeymoon and various holiday excursions, we came up with the idea of renting it out as a guest house. Why build a permanent dwelling in a beautiful space when you can just drive there and park up. The result is minimal impact and an easy come, easy go lifestyle.'

lovestruck

style notes

What started out as a spartan space, albeit with the advantage of lovely warm wood surfaces, has been artfully and instinctively converted into this rustic mobile home.

Everything added looks at home here – the reclaimed stained glass windows, wooden cupboards and surfaces, and mis-matched, hand-painted vases. Floors have been softened with a number of worn ethnic rugs, a goatskin rug and textured cushion enhance a well-loved Lloyd Loom chair and the otherwise uncompromising wooden bed platform is made inviting with a simple dressing of quality white cotton sheets and a goosedown duvet. Nearly everything here is a cast-off but it would be hard not to find this space a restful, simple arcadia.

The inspiration and setting for one of Roald Dahl's most famous children's stories (*Danny the Champion of the World*) came from this charming, sky-blue gypsy caravan. Danny and his father lived in '...a real old gypsy wagon with big wheels and fine patterns all over it.' The caravan currently stands in the garden of the late author's home underneath the treehouse.

Roald Dahl's sister had acquired the wagon in the 1950s and he took it over in 1960. He bought it mainly for his children to use as a playhouse and as the years passed, his grandchildren used it, too. It has obviously been well loved by all and has been kept in an immaculate condition. It shows that a caravan does not have to be taken a great distance – if any at all. Like Roald Dahl's gypsy wagon, it doesn't matter if its resting place is just yards from the house, it is still somewhere to escape to.

roald dahl

style notes

With a highly decorative exterior and similarly elaborate interior, this caravan has naturally become a place of imagination, a world away from reality.

You can dream, drift, write and read when there is enough 'fairytale' surrounding you. Such fussiness may appear distracting but isn't. The quality of the structure and paintwork is enhanced by a few basic items inside – some tin mugs, a plain glass jar of wild flowers and pretty but simple curtains – all ensure that your thoughts can wander freely.

frank's

The origins of this caravan are a little unclear. Current owner Frank purchased it from a friend when tent camping lost its appeal.

It is believed to be made from the fuselage section of a World War II aircraft mounted onto a car chassis. The quirky additions of a felt roof, porch and bay window make this caravan unique, as Frank quickly realised when he took it to a festival: 'I took this caravan to the Goodwood Revival one year and I was swamped with interest, almost to the point of exhaustion! In the end I had to escape from the unrelenting questions and go for a walk.'

'Upon my return I found a small envelope pushed under the door. Inside were several photos of my caravan at different stages of restoration. A phone number accompanied it but even to this day, when I have called the number, no-one answers, so the mystery of who built it still remains unsolved.'

style notes

This is a delightfully simple space, filled with almost incidental items from different periods of Frank's life. The items may be small but they are of great personal significance – a few brass buttons from an old uniform, a felt badge of sergeant's stripes with frayed edges, a vintage box of matches and a coarse woven blanket long past its issue date. It's the integrity of these items that enhances this unique space.

old shepherd's hut

During the 1950s and '60s this shepherd's hut was used by John Pearce while he was working as a gamekeeper in Dorset. 'Before the arrival of electric heaters, game birds were reared and hatched using broody domestic hens. After hatching, the broodies and chicks were put into coops on a rearing field,' explains John, 'the keeper's hut was towed to the field together with feed and any other kit that was needed. There was a bunk bed in the hut as we had to stay to protect the birds day and night from predators.'

With two hatchings of chicks, rearing duties lasted from May through to August when the birds would be able to look after themselves. 'Due to the length of time we were expected to carry out our duties, a tent would just not do. The shepherd's hut gave us a sense of home and although it was small, it was enough.'

style notes

Life doesn't get much simpler than this – somewhere to rest your head and shelter from the worst of the weather, with just a few functional items. Through meticulous and considered restoration the original woodwork has been repaired in a thoughtful and responsible way and the paintwork suitably matched, in tone and effect, with a subtle touch.

new shepherd's hut

'My wife and I were intrigued by an ancient shepherd's hut which stood on the brow of a hill, just a few miles away from our home,' comments Richard. 'Shepherd's huts have stood gently fading away and almost forgotten for many years. They were just part of a countryman's peripheral vision in a way. Yet each one has a history to be told by a local who remembers it being towed out to the downs for lambing and then playing in it as children when the hut returned to the farmyard.'

'One day, in 2000, the hut disappeared on a lorry and we really regretted not finding out more about it. Soon after, we decided to try and build our own. We purchased an old chassis from a West Dorset farmer and set about building a hut based on original designs from a long-gone foundry in Wiltshire.' 'We very much relish retreating to our hut when time allows. Not much beats watching the sun sink over the stable door or watching the house martins swoop low over the pond near to where it stands.'

style notes

Being built to order, a new shepherd's hut can be customised according to your taste. This one is positioned in the garden, beside a historic Dorset watermeadow, described by Thomas Hardy in *Far from the Madding Crowd*. 'The river slid along noiselessly as a shade, the swelling reeds and sedge forming a flexible palisade upon its moist brink.'

This simple sanctuary has tongue and groove walls, lovely oak flooring and a comfortable sofabed for guests. Beside the woodburning stove is a pile of logs and a kettle sits ready for use. A few mementoes customise the space – a horseshoe, a watercolour postcard and a candlelit lantern. Such is the special location of the hut and its inherent charm that only a few simple human comforts are needed.

trailer park treasures

Popular with people from all walks of life and endorsed and used by celebrities during their 'heydays', trailer parks were seen by many as a way to solve the burgeoning housing shortage of the 1950s.

In the early 1950s, the actor Bing Crosby was busy funding and designing his own architectural vision of a luxury 'state of the art' trailer park. In 1955, when 'Blue Skies Village' opened in Rancho Mirage, near Palm Springs, USA, many of Bing's Hollywood friends visited and endorsed his new venture. With its palm tree-lined streets named and dedicated to film stars of the era, glitzy mobile homes and caravans placed on manicured plots, the future seemed rosy for the trailer park.

In subsequent years, however, the affordability of trailer housing meant that the parks became viewed as low income housing for those on the poverty line rather than as desirable holiday homes and their popularity declined. Many amazing trailers were left to decay gracefully along with the dreams of earlier visionaries.

But when something is so deeply instilled in popular American culture it is perhaps inevitable that a legacy will live on in one way or another – and indeed it has today with the 'trailer park' style.

A resurgence in popularity has brought many trailers out of retirement, restored and back on show with all their colourful brash 1950s and '60s design. The exteriors with their polished aluminium, horizontal panelling or painted graphics are as flamboyant as the kitsch interior décor. Trailer park style is not about conforming; it's about bringing your own personality into the design. This very liberating style leaves you free to experiment with colour, textures and personal items as pretty much anything goes.

canned ham

A love of classic cars, but not of camping under canvas, eventually inspired owner Stephen to find his own cool caravan. 'Having spent years attending hot rod and classic car shows and spending nights sleeping in a tent, it was time to buy a caravan! Loving all things 1940s and 1950s we originally looked at buying a period British-made caravan, but after seeing all the various types of American "Travel Trailers" nothing less would do,' claims Stephen.

'We purchased it from Santa Rosa, California, via an internet auction in August 2006. Our 1954 Cardinal Travel Trailer, or "canned ham" as it is known due to its shape, was in an original but battered condition. An endless list of jobs followed which included rubbing it down, stripping the paint, replacing the glass and sourcing period fabrics and accessories which brought it to its present condition. Since 2007, we have used the caravan at car shows across the country and for holidays. It's towed behind our 1940s' Dodge Pick-up truck and everyone who sees it seems to love it as much as we do.'

style notes

The owners wanted to restore this neglected trailer in keeping with its original style. The three key elements to the success of a project like this is knowing when to stop, ensuring that the restoration work is carried out to a very high standard, and thinking and looking carefully at original colours, tones and materials.

The result here has integrity – things have been repaired where necessary and thorough research carried out to source appropriate materials. For instance, the tone of the vinyl used to re-cover the seats is perfect, as is the colour of the vintage barkcloth used for cushions. The owners have managed to hold back from over-doing and creating a rose-tinted vision of what would have been there.

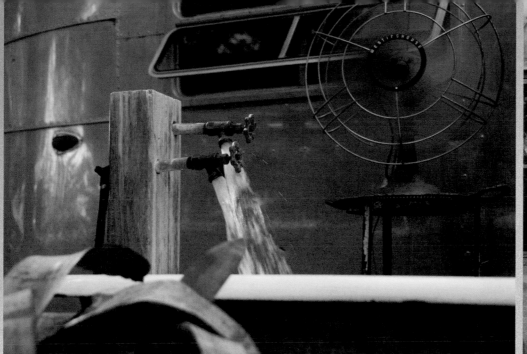

Alone in a Texan field with Johnson grass growing up around the wheels and the added humiliation of locals taking pot shots at her, this 1961 Avion caravan was destined for a sorry ending until musician, artist and writer Sam Baker spotted it for sale.

Sam comments, 'I asked the vendor why it was being sold and it turned out that the owner had no use for it any more and he wanted it to go to a good home before it suffered any more abuse – the vendor reassured me that it was not stolen and had the papers to prove it.' Sam quickly secured a cash deal and the trailer was his.

'It turned out that 'Shiney' (its nickname for obvious reasons) was not too willing to leave the field where she had been taking root for many years,' adds Sam. 'It took several attempts to pry her away from the weeds and move her to her new home in the woods. Shiney is happy here – especially as no-one shoots at her now.'

style notes

One major joy of caravanning is finding a quiet location, with the privacy this brings and the opportunity to engage in the outdoor life. The final resting place of this hard-living Avion is in a secluded woody area in the grounds of the owners' house. Finding and plumbing in a period rolltop bath and building a decked area from reclaimed wood have created a very personal space. The native yuccas, the red of the vintage porch chair and classic desk fan are all part of creating the mood, and make sense in the searing heat of Texas summers. It illustrates south-western style, the pleasures of your own environment after a day's toil, and how the well travelled trailer and its owner have finally found a comfortable home.

avion

carefree commander

This splendid Carefree Commander was built in 1958 in Victoria, Australia by Carefree Caravans. Current owner John purchased the caravan in 2008 and set about re-painting the exterior along with some personalised sign-writing to give it a retro facelift. 'The interior was in remarkable condition for its age but I still made some minor cosmetic changes. I like the van because it represents a simpler life from days gone by, and to me, it is home,' says John.

Judging by the stickers on it, the van has been around Australia several times already, but nonetheless John is confident she's capable of doing it again.

'I now have a caravan equally as capable as any modern version for much less money and it is a real head-turner too! The caravan is towed by my 1976 Holden, making the outfit very "Australian".'

style notes

The benefit of keeping clutter under control in a small space is obvious. This isn't a boring space by any means – the beer mats and labels use every inch of ceiling space, but the key is the orderly way in which they are positioned in horizontal lines. If you look closely you will see that their sizes have been taken into consideration, too, with smaller labels positioned along the edges and larger ones more centrally. This creates a stunning effect, allowing the caravan to appear orderly, yet at the same time keeping a host of memories on show for its young owner.

Shasta made mobile homes and travel trailers for well over 60 years. They started out making trailer homes for the US armed forces in 1941 and by the mid-1950s the boom in mobile homes and travel trailers in the States was in full swing. The Shasta brand was one of the most popular in the USA due to its good value and low price: the public couldn't get enough.

Shasta was renowned for its stylish interiors and exteriors, and most people associate the distinctive wings and bold coloured stripes that were placed on each side of the trailers with the brand. This bold styling was introduced to the range around the late 1950s.

Sadly, with no apparent goodbye, Shasta trailers, with their distinctive styling, seemed to all but disappear along with the brand in the latter half of the twentieth century. However, in 2008, a retro but modern Shasta Airflyte caravan with a 'state of the art' interior and trademark identifying wings, was re-introduced onto the market.

shasta

style notes

This Shasta has a sense of joyousness and fun – the external design elements of the space-age, sci fi-shaped fin, the red and white zig zag and the louvered windows. It's a bit like a diner on wheels, and the internal decoration should follow suit. Keep the colours strong, put garlands of exotic silk flowers around the door, source models of funky vintage cars of the period such as the Nash Metropolitan, and some old diner signs and enjoy...

jewel

Before being shipped to the UK, this 1957 Jewel caravan had to undertake a 1000-mile journey to Portland, Oregon, the nearest overseas shipping port. Owner Cliff and his family purchased the caravan three years ago from Wendy, at The Tin Inn Travel Trailer Company, who specialise in affordable vintage American caravans.

'We wanted a trailer that would complement our 1967 Ford Mustang and it's turned out to be the perfect partnership,' comments Cliff.

'We have owned British caravans but much prefer the American style. We love the quirkiness and character that comes in abundance with American caravans – which sets them apart from the rest. We did have a 1952 Airstream Flying Cloud but we sold it in order to buy the Jewel.'

'We spend a lot of time together as a family going to various American shows all over the country; the kids love it, we meet great people and have a lot of fun.'

style notes

Using colour and pattern appropriately sets the mood. The optimistic primrose yellow of the original cooker and fridge door and the pale blue of the worktop and table surfaces hark back to the optimism of the 1950s and '60s. It's the evocation of an idealised sunny and good-humoured life.

Keeping small accessories such as the pans in similar tones and of classic design, adding red through the gingham curtains and melamine crockery, further celebrate the modernity and vibrancy of that period.

'Original Teardrop caravans in good condition, or to a style of my liking, are rarer than hens' teeth,' explains Paul. 'I've always wanted to own one but after years of fruitless searching I decided that making one myself was the only option.' It took a thousand hours of dedicated work over three summers to complete this hand-built replica of an American 1940s Teardrop caravan.

'My first trip was by invitation to the Goodwood Festival to celebrate 100 years of caravanning. Each morning mine would take to the racing circuit for a leisurely lap to open the day's racing.'

'We use the Teardrop mainly as sleeping quarters for the music festivals that I attend and play at, as I'm a professional drummer. The caravan is also handy to put the drum kit in en-route if there's not enough room in the back of my 1950s pick-up truck.'

teardrop

style notes

The caravan is compact by anyone's standard – it's only 4 foot wide, 4 foot high and 8 foot long. 'Inside there's enough room to sleep two with comfort. The cooking facilities, however, are al fresco in the rear kitchen,' remarks Caroline, Paul's partner.

If, like Paul, you have a strong affinity to an earlier period, your pursuit of all things from that era dictate your style. It is an admirable feat to recreate a period piece as accurately as Paul's Teardrop.

british classics

A few legendary caravan brands such as Carlight, Cheltenham, Winchester and Safari, attained classic status in the post-war years. These brands cost up to four times more than other regular caravans. However, there was a market among wealthy buyers who were prepared to spend such amounts to own a desirable 'name'. This enabled these manufacturers to lead the way with quality design.

Carlight, in particular, is considered the 'king of kings' brand. The company invested large sums in research and development and employed highly skilled workers to develop new techniques of caravan manufacture and construction.

The design of these classic caravans often followed a distinctive shape which became identified with the brand, such as the use of a lantern roof, with only minor modifications over time to follow the vagaries of fashion. Subtle construction methods, such as no visible screw heads on the exterior surfaces, contributed to their streamlined and quality appearance. Subconsciously these caravans looked and felt as high end as their production values.

The examples in this chapter all feature classic exteriors and fabulous wooden furniture and quality fittings inside. For the most part the interiors are unchanged and have been restored only where necessary. This minimal restoration, along with the quality of original materials and workmanship, has introduced these iconic brands to a new audience, who appreciate the high spec interiors that include cocktail cabinets, bespoke china and top of the range kitchen equipment.

Carlight is the only one of these manufacturers still in business today. Their caravans have longevity and well-maintained models are sought after and treasured.

carlight continental

'When I was about 10 years old, I remember going to a local caravan dealer along with my parents to look at a Carlight Continental,' recalls owner Dave. 'It was like nothing I had ever seen before. My father had always aspired to owning one, but due to certain circumstances at the time, he couldn't really afford one.'

'However, my wife Sally and I bought a two-berth 1975 Carlight soon after we met. When our first child Alyssa was born and we needed more space, we purchased this classic 1972.'

It took 18 months for Dave and Sally to finish the restoration, during which time they took it to the Carlight factory in Sleaford and had it re-finished in the original white paint. The caravan is now used through the summer months for rallies, holidays and shows.

'We love the character that the old classic caravans have; they are so well built and each has its own individuality. My father is proud with the work we have done on the restoration, and I feel in some way that I have achieved his dream.'

style notes

From the 1930s onwards high-end caravans began being supplied with their own branded crockery sets and were also rented out fully equipped. The crockery is now highly sought after. Carlight, regarded by many as the most enduring quality brand, supplied its caravans with their own branded crockery. To keep it safe during transit, kitchen cupboards were designed to store the bone china securely. As they were top of the range caravans they were also supplied with purpose-built cocktail cabinets. There are no plastic beakers here – real glasses are kept secure with wooden cut outs to hold the stems securely in transit.

Quality of the level of this meticulously restored caravan is rarely seen. It also boasts top of the range Wilton carpet with springy underlay, immaculate paintwork and upholstery. There is no nod to fashion here, just an acknowledgement of this amazing brand and the unpretentious quality of the caravan itself.

the royal caravan

The Caravan Club presented this 'one of a kind' caravan to Prince Charles and Princess Anne when they were children in 1955. Although it was intended just for use by the Royal children, the caravan is fully roadworthy and functional. The Duke of Edinburgh, who is patron of The Caravan Club, is said to have towed the caravan with a Hillman Husky shortly after taking delivery of it.

The 1/3rd scale caravan was built by Rollalong Limited of Ringwood, a well-known caravan manufacturer during the 1950s, using traditional construction techniques. It has undergone several refurbishments over the years, most recently when it was completely restored by the original makers to coincide with The Caravan Club's centenary in 2007. It is now a very popular exhibit at the National Motor Museum in Beaulieu, Hampshire.

style notes
This play caravan is a fabulous miniature example, in perfect working order. The cooker isn't functional, but the sink, oak bureau and everything else in the caravan can be used. A tartan blanket, a few cushions and a classic teddy bear furnish it – now all it needs is some children and their imagination.

'Style never goes out of fashion and our Safari always attracts a group of admirers wherever we go,' explains Caroline. 'Fascinated caravanners often ask about our Safari, have a look around, and are amazed by the fact that everything is in such wonderful condition for a caravan built in 1979. They usually end up staying to dinner as Steve, my husband and chef, produces delicious meals from locally-bought produce.'

'"Towed Hall" as we have affectionately named her, is among the last Safaris produced. The irony is that they were too well-made and it proved impossible to make a profit without compromising on quality. That our van is still in such good order is a tribute to the skill of the craftsmen who lovingly built her.'

The Safari was the choice of those who knew quality when they saw it. It was the caravan to aspire to – even the flash of colour on the caravan was sprayed to match the owner's car.

safari 14/2

style notes

The upholstery fabric used here may strike terror into the hearts of some people, yet be a source of decorating inspiration for others. Its dense textural quality and dominant design was considered luxurious and modern in its time. If the condition is still reasonable it can look good left alone. Soft furnishings can be added to complement the upholstery, using the key colours of the fabric and the paintwork, both interior and exterior, but always allow the original fabric to set the tone.

Vintage recipe books hint at the owner's occupation and the illustrations and typography on the book covers look perfectly at home alongside the fabric for the sofa and cushions.

organic

Characterized by their organic soft curves, the caravans in this chapter represent a conscious movement towards modernism.

These caravans still look modern by today's standards, even though the designs date from the mid-1950s – the time of the Cold War, the development of the space race, the launch of Sputnik and the Festival of Britain. Following the privations of World War II, designers were looking boldly to the future in their technology and designs.

The designs did not always prove popular with the public, particularly in Britain where a more reserved exterior shape was popular.

Today, though, these caravans look attractively contemporary. Their use of moulded fibreglass and large wraparound windows give a futuristic shape and brightness, a world away from the more traditional shapes available in the 1950s. The idiosyncratic Swedish-designed, egg-shaped form of the SMV, with its body of riveted aluminium, and the beautifully curvy Dutch Biod, have clearly stood the test of time.

biod

'As we became older and softer, we made a gentle progression from motorcycle camping to classic campervan ownership,' says Adam. 'This was followed by a growing fascination with lightweight classic caravans. We had already owned three different classic caravans before we saw pictures of a Biod Extase on the internet.'

Its appearance, diminutive size and practical fibreglass construction reflected everything that Adam desired in a caravan but due to the rarity of the model, it took Adam many searches, and a lot of patience, to find the right one. 'It took three years of scanning Dutch auction sites, along with some logistical and linguistic challenges, before we finally purchased our caravan. It has now become an integral part of our lives.'

style notes

The curvy rounded form of the biod provides a sense of cocooning comfort but creates its own challenges such as how to hang curtains around a curved and convex shape.

The curtain issue was addressed by using curtain wires in lines across the full width of the windows to keep the fabric in place. The rounded exterior of the caravan is echoed in the decorative items to create a sense of continuity and comfort. The vintage tableware and table re-covered with a modern re-issue of period formica, mixed in with modern funky coloured pieces, are all in keeping with the progressive design of this caravan.

Peter was looking for a caravan as a winter project. However, there was one important criterion – it would have to compliment 'Lindy', his beloved 1950 Series One Land Rover. After several months of searching far and wide, he found a Willerby just a stone's throw away from home. Unfortunately, it was in a sorry state and needed immediate restoration work. 'Luckily a good friend of mine is an ex-army mechanic, so for king and country, and with pride in our hearts, we set about getting this unique caravan back on the road,' says Peter.

'The restoration involved a lot of work on the chassis and even more painstaking work on the fibreglass exterior. Friends and family were kept busy using sewing machines to finish off the cushions and a local craftsman restored the cabinets. I have to say that this project was more than I had expected, but it's been worth it. Although I'm not sure I would do it again!'

willerby vogue

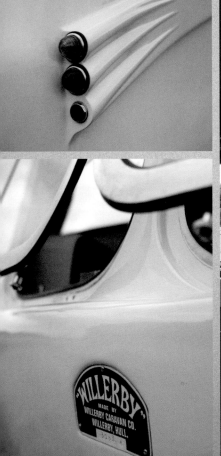

style notes

Sometimes you have an item of such rarity and beauty that the only respectful thing to do is to restore and re-furbish the interior as close to the original as possible. In this case the job took the owner nine months of weekends and evenings. The attention to detail and resourcefulness are all too apparent. The original gas lights were converted to electricity and the interior and exterior have been restored. The cooker and sink are original but the oak veneering on the cupboard doors, which fits onto the original moulded fibreglass cupboards, has been completely re-made, making this caravan not just beautiful but museum worthy too.

Having the technical know-how when it comes to restoring a vintage caravan is always an advantage and it is certainly the case with this caravan.

A craftsman by trade, SMV-10 owner Edward uses his talent to restore vintage Citroëns. Like so many other classic car owners, a caravan was the next thing on his wish list!

'The shape of the SMV is what first attracted me,' he explains, 'and it's a perfect companion for my beloved Citroën.

Although the caravan was in a reasonable condition when he purchased it, Edward decided to put his skills and talent to good use by removing the interior and refurbishing it to an extremely high standard.

'It's a real creative release owning a caravan,' comments Edward, 'collecting all the accessories is a big part of the experience.'

smv-10

style notes

Being able to visualise what you are looking for rather than taking the easy option and buying new can pay handsome dividends.

The owner of this SMV was refurbishing the interior when he noticed two old kitchen curtains belonging to a friend with a palette and style that would work perfectly with the orange and yellow interior. The fabric design was by chance a classic piece of textile design from 1964, a piece of vintage Heals fabric called 'Water meadow', designed by Colleen Farr, who also designed textiles for Liberty.

The theme continues with a 1960s stackable coffee table with a striking tiled top, an internet find he couldn't resist.

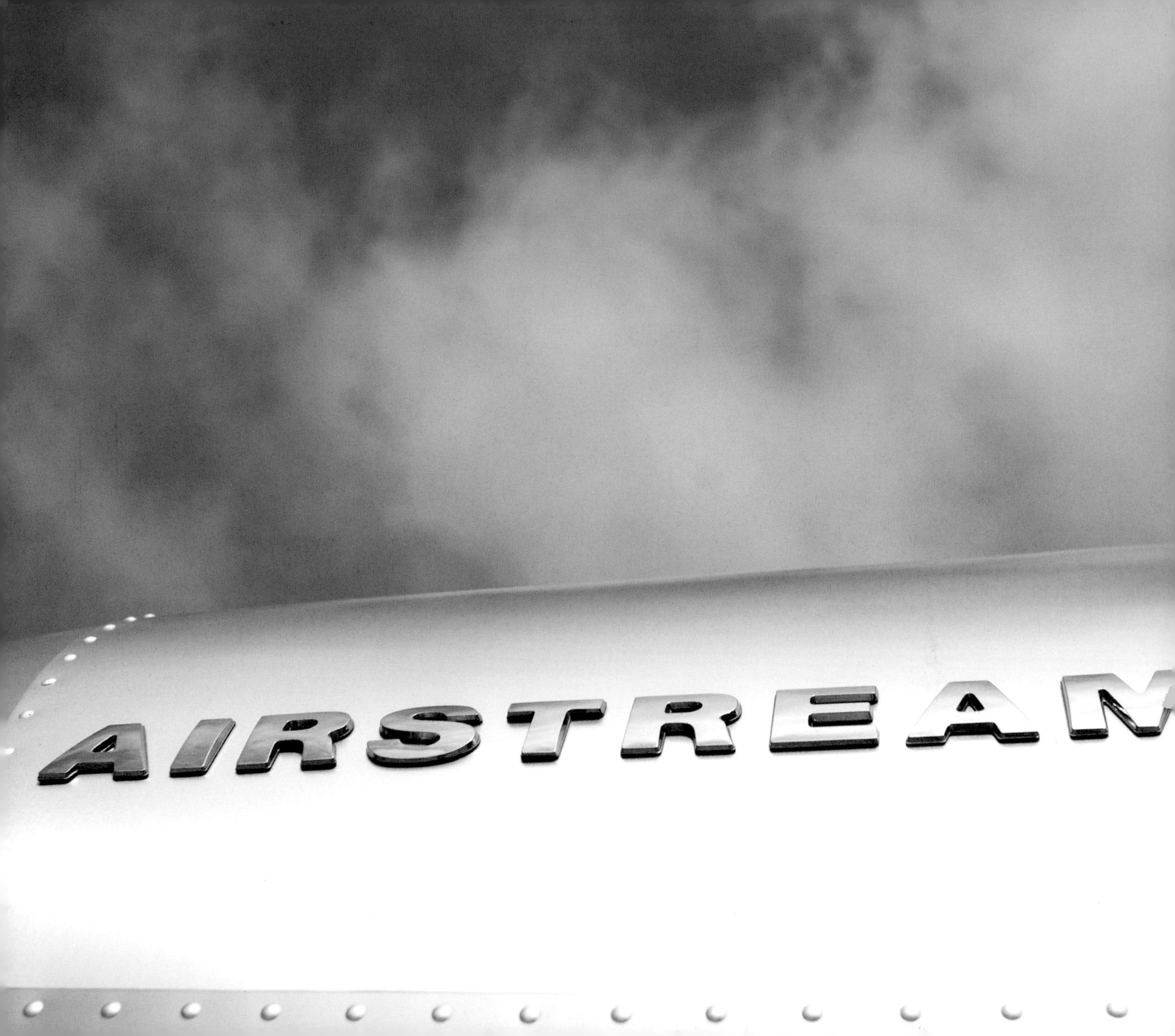
AIRSTREAM

silver bullets

'One of those silver bullet things' is usually how people identify these American design icons. Most people will recognise Airstreams from their streamline shape and shiny aluminium exterior, even if they do not know them by name or have any interest in caravanning.

The Airstream caravan first hit the road in the 1930s. It was constructed using monocoque aviation technology and is very similar to an aircraft fuselage. The exterior styling pays homage to other groundbreaking transportation of the era – airships, trains and cars.

The Airstream achieved global recognition in 1969 when the Apollo 11 astronauts returned to earth after their momentous landing on the moon and were housed in one. This was a fitting choice of accommodation as pioneer and founder of Airstream Wally Byam believed we should all 'see more, do more, live more.'

Over the decades the Airstream's exterior design has retained its distinctive exposed rivets and segmented panels, but its style has also developed to reflect the changing influences of each era.

The interior is where most owners express their creative streak, and ideas run amok with limitless themes that are as diverse and interesting as the owners themselves. Some owners choose to work with a blank canvas and remove the interior completely to start afresh; whereas others enhance the original interiors with a particular style from the year of their caravan.

One wonders if Wally Byam would have ever dreamt that Airstreams would become the fashionable design icons that they are today.

custom airstream

Mark Hutchinson was introduced to Airstreams in 2002 following a first camping holiday with his young children. 'We were in a tent which had a leak in it and typically it just didn't stop raining.'

'Despite the hiccups it was great fun and we all agreed that we wanted to brave the great outdoors again, only not in a tent! A caravan seemed like a good idea, but the kids wanted "retro", so we toyed with the idea of a VW Split Screen. It was while we were checking them out on the internet that we came across Airstreams.'

'We found a specialist dealer, Sarah Jane, and within a few months became the owners of a 1962 22-foot Safari. It was truly magnificent and whilst the towing was initially daunting, we used it a lot.'

'The opportunity then presented itself to purchase this 1958 20-foot Custom. Being one of only ten ever built it truly is an Airstream with a unique aura; it feels like you are in a time warp, especially with the picture of John Wayne we have on the wall. All the original features are still in place, including gas fitments and the dark wooden panelling, which makes it feel so warm.'

style notes

If you are lucky enough to own a caravan with original fittings and furniture like this wonderful example, it is easy to add finishing touches.

The trick is to look for items that echo the period of the caravan. They don't have to be from exactly the same date as colours, tones and shapes tend to come in and out of fashion.

In this case the warm gold of the 1960s soda siphon, the early '70s bargello-style cushion cover, the bargain amber Perspex coffee cups from a charity shop and the gently curved Thermos coffee jug all harmonise with the already authentic interior.

land yacht

You never know what to expect when purchasing a vintage caravan and it's always advisable to check for possible problems before buying. This can be tricky, however, when the caravan is several thousands of miles away. When this Airstream Safari came up for sale online in Ohio, USA, it was a high risk option for owner and co-author of this book, Chris Haddon.

'I instantly fell in love with the caravan,' says Chris. 'After weighing up the pros and cons, and after several phone calls to a shipping company, I was confident it was possible to buy it and arrange for delivery to England... all from the comfort of my armchair.'

Not much had changed from the original. 'I'm a child of the 1970s,' explains Chris, 'so I love the fake wood veneer and the abundance of plastic. I have softened the macho look at the request of my partner with fabrics and accessories. We now use the Airstream almost as a static caravan and escape there as much as we can with children and dog in tow.'

style notes

Because of their shape, Airstream trailers provide a relatively long space and can be a series of adjoining rooms. When spaces link together like this it is good to have some harmonising features. Things don't have to match, but here, for example, the relaxed stripe of the mismatched crochet bedcovers echoes the stripe of the under-sink curtains and the cushions on the sofa. Once you have achieved this sense of harmony, you can have fun adding personal touches such as a happy mix of odd pillowcases, sheets and duvet covers. The result is a comfortable, modern Woodstock, folksy look.

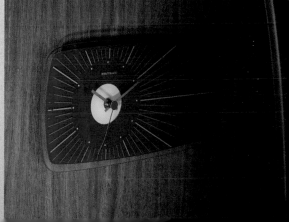

'My first experience of caravanning was not cool,' explains Viscount Coke. 'My grandmother had an old static caravan at beautiful Mother Ivey's Bay near Padstow. As small children we played with other children on the campsite and ran amok in the warm sun, although we had learnt to appreciate outdoor life as a family before this when our parents regularly took us on camping holidays.'

'Now I have a family with four children, ranging in ages from ten to three years old. The best holidays we have are not those in a luxury hotel, but ones where we take the Airstream off on expeditions. We enjoy the simple pleasures, such as taking it to beautiful places, being in the open air and doing things together, like playing with the dogs on the beach.'

'You know you've got it right when your six-year-old son exclaims during a breakfast BBQ: "this is the best ever breakfast, Dad". It is these memories I want my children to have and what better place to have them in than in our 1965 22-foot Airstream Safari, an inspired fortieth birthday present from my wife.'

international

style notes

This interior mixes just about every element – colour, texture and pattern – and the result is a lovely contrast to the polished, streamlined exterior. Using Mexico and the painter Frida Kahlo as inspiration, the fridge and cupboards have been adorned with iconic colourful images; the seating is re-covered in a multi-coloured, striped, hard-wearing fabric; and the dividing curtain is an embroidered patchwork, vintage bedspread. The mixture of strong colours, patterns, Mexican artefacts and graphic colourful imagery of Mexico and the southwest states of the US have created a truly original space for this happy, busy family.

airstream bambi

This modern European Airstream Bambi 422 is ideal for those who want the 'cool' element of caravanning, without the need to travel around with a tool kit to carry out running repairs. It has the charm of a vintage Airstream but with the modern and reliable conveniences of a 21st-century caravan. This particular range was designed for European roads and their more compact tow cars. The design also had to allow for European restrictions on caravan sizes and weights. The award-winning designer responsible for the look of the new European Airstream fleet has also given the interior a wow factor with ultra-modern, luxurious detailing.

style notes

Sometimes a trailer requires very little in the way of extra styling. 'Simple' just works. The immaculate aluminium exterior, the neat form of the shell and the slick internal fittings all speak for themselves. Red, black and white are used as small decorative touches – they can be changed, updated or personalised easily. The clever interior space, with its modern design features, means that within a few minutes of arriving at your destination you can be up and running.

recycled

Lessening our impact on the planet is now a major priority in our lives – caravanning is no exception. More and more people are realising that caravanning is not only cool but can help them reduce their global footprint by shunning overseas holidays in favour of staying in their own countries.

An old forgotten caravan or vehicle can be recycled, made over, then used for a number of different purposes – an office at home; a studio in the garden; a child's playhouse; or, as was originally intended, for holidays. Styling your caravan to your own taste does not have to be expensive either – a cool caravan can be achieved on a thrifty budget.

Caravanning can be 'green' as well as economic. All the basic daily necessities can be addressed in one way or another – solar panels can be used to generate the power for the few electrical appliances, a wood-burning stove can be used for cooking, to provide warmth and heating and some caravan owners even collect and re-use rainwater.

Fabrics can be recycled and used for upholstery. Old flooring, cabinets and doors can also be customised and reused to renovate an interior.

Turning unexpected or recycled objects into workable features ofen gives items a new lease of life beyond their intended original use and proves that one person's junk is another person's treasure.

ecostream

The Caravan Club set itself a brief to design and build an environmentally-friendly caravan to put the 'green' into caravanning.

The Club started with a European Airstream 534 and set to work installing a wealth of energy-saving features and recycled materials. Hot water is delivered courtesy of a wood-burning stove and stored in a Harley Davidson fuel tank.

Power for the caravan is delivered via roof-mounted solar panels, which in turn power the LED low-energy lighting system.

A reclaimed underground water pipe for the shower tray, bamboo flooring and a composting toilet may not be on your standard caravan specification but this model brilliantly demonstrates the ingenuity that can be applied to every feature. It is still lavish and luxurious, but most importantly it's eco-friendly.

style notes

Having the ethos defined at the start of a project provides a clear guide for the interior dressing. The ecostream features recycled and re-purposed items throughout.

The wood-burning stove is surrounded by a mismatching but complementary grouping of Victorian tiles sourced from a Manchester reclamation yard; old lockers from a refurbished police station function as kitchen cupboards.

Once the theme and colour palette are established, you have clear guidelines for incorporating smaller items. The tea lights in re-used coloured jars, earthenware Meakin crockery from the 1970s in lime and yellow green colours and vintage-coloured seagrass place mats continue the earnest but stylish theme. The cushion covers made from colour co-ordinated retro fabrics and a stool made from a recycled tin drum from India provide the finishing touches.

eco farmers

'For 50 years my husband Richie's grandparents have owned a fruit and vegetable farm in Bowie, Texas,' explains Cortny. 'When grandpa, who at the time was 82, had to have shoulder surgery, it fell on us to up sticks and move to the farm to help out.'

'Our hearts were set on purchasing a vintage caravan which we could restore and make our own. There was one criteria – it had to be aluminium and look cool. By chance we stumbled across a 1982 Avion caravan and instantly fell in love with it.

The original interior was designed around one colour palette – brown! If they could have tinted the windows brown they would have,' adds Cortny. 'One of the first things we installed was a window-height bed so we can gaze out at the far-reaching views.'

style notes

In a small space, decoration based on one dominant graphic element often helps define the style. The focus of this modern log cabin-style interior is the dinette upholstery which has been re-covered in a strong, large-scale houndstooth fabric by a textile designer friend. It sets the scene and allows other items such as the guitar and artwork to hold their own against white walls.

The simple solution to bathroom storage – recycling wooden boxes – allows otherwise inconsequential, everyday objects such as shells, a favourite necklace or photograph to be displayed artfully. Working on a muddy farm imposed its own problems, so the floors were covered with recycled horse stall mats, making them durable and easy to clean.

'As a teenager, several of my friends started to convert trucks and buses into mobile homes so they could frequent festivals dotted around the country,' says Daisy. 'The freedom appealed to me but it was only when my rented house was sold to developers and ultimately demolished that I had the push to follow in their tracks.'

Ten years have now passed since acquiring her first caravan and Daisy has thrown herself into the 'new travellers' way of life. 'My life tends to follow the seasons; the autumn months are spent fruit picking while the winter months are for weaving. This then leaves late spring and the summer months free for the many festivals I attend along with my caravans, a coach built 1954 Brampton and this 1980s Roma. It's not so much about a cheaper way of life, it's more about the quality of life. Where possible we get power from solar panels and collect rain water, it's very low impact living.'

'Whatever I own has to be practical, as after all, it is my home and there is no room for superfluous items.'

daisy

style notes

Daisy has a passion for natural dyes and textiles, weaving and an environmentally conscious lifestyle which are reflected in the styling of her caravan. The blankets on her bed were woven by her and dyed using local native plants. The looms are kept in a studio elsewhere, but smaller items can be made by hand or on a sewing machine.

Inspirational images adorn the walls in this formica-clad old showman's caravan. With its fairylights and wood-burning stove, it is both a highly decorative and cosy space.

Surrounding yourself with items of your own making gives a natural harmony to the style – your taste in colours, textures and visual effects all combining to create a united look.

globetrotter

'Due to the ever-rising noise levels from my children, an office in the garden seemed the ideal solution,' comments Chris, co-author of this book.

'I had looked at elaborate sheds to convert into an office but I really wanted something a bit different from the norm. So I started looking around at the possibility of buying an Airstream and converting it into my work space.'

'I found this 1963 Globetrotter for sale in Connecticut, USA. It was perfect and after a lot of effort, trying to convince the owners that I was totally serious and I really did want to ship it over to England, it finally arrived.'

'Now my journey to work consists of opening the back door and walking a few yards to my office; good news for the environment, too, as now my global footprint is just a few steps from house to caravan.'

During the winter months a large Labrador can be found sprawled in front of the wood-burning stove, wallowing in the heat.

style notes

A home office positioned in your garden is often a dream, and this caravan definitely provides a working environment with all modern facilities.

Re-covering the sofa in a modern Osborne and Little print that echoes the filigree spot detail of the light fittings provides a subtle visual link that helps to harmonise the space. Velveteen cushions add spot colour and texture while a collection of vintage American signs, items of the graphic design trade and old toys add charm. The vintage items sit happily alongside the top-of-range computer equipment creating a modern but not clinical environment for working and meeting clients.

'Everyone smiles when we drive past. It's such an amazing vehicle!' announces Emily Chalmers, owner of this 1967 Citroën H Van.

citroën h van

'My husband is the designated driver, due to the H Van's visibility and steering column issues,' adds Emily, stylist and proprietor of London interiors shop, Caravan. The H Van gives Emily and husband Chris a chance to escape the urban bustle and go on weekend road trips.

'I've always loved H vans and when we had the opportunity to buy one we both jumped at the chance. This one had a slightly unusual background as it was previously a mortician's vehicle in Paris, but we were undeterred so went ahead and purchased it. A previous owner had done the hard work and already partly converted the van, so I did what I love best and styled the interior to my own unique taste.'

style notes

The idiosyncratic personal touches in this vintage H van are a clear acknowledgement of its talented interior stylist owner, Emily. This is a confident, individual space, dressed with humour and a sense of design history.

The caravan exudes true confidence, with links made between different design fabric prints, traditional and modern pictures, real items and découpage, a strong use of colour and a mixture of purely decorative and practical items.

This van is truly multi-functional, working as an office, spare guest room, showcase, holiday accommodation and vehicle.

sourcebook

donna flower
Beautiful antique and vintage textiles. From 19th-century French fabrics
to the vintage-inspired fabrics of today.
www.donnaflower.com

lucy bates vintage fabric
Fabrics from the golden age of British design.
110 High Street, Ashwell
Hertfordshire SG7 5NS
Tel: 01462 742905   www.lucybatesvintagefabric.co.uk

secondhand rose
Thousands of original vintage wallpaper and linoleum patterns.
230 5th Avenue suite No 510
New York, NY 10001, USA
Tel: 001 212 393 9002   www.secondhandrose.com

reprodepot
Reproductions of vintage and retro fabrics, for upholstery, dressmaking and crafts. Also dressmaking patterns and haberdashery.
www.reprodepot.com

fabrics galore
Ends of lines from designers and bargain finds for usual and unusual fabrics.
54 Lavender Hill
London SW11 5RH
www.fabricsgalore.co.uk

brent plastics
Plastic laminate sheeting in a multitude of styles and colours.
Unit D Cobbold Estate, Cobbold Road
Willesden NW10 9BP
Tel: 020 8451 0100   www.brentplastics.co.uk

caravan style
Quirky interiors shop, owned by interior stylist and author Emily Chalmers.
3 Redchurch Street, Shoreditch
London E2 7DJ   www.caravanstyle.com

hungerford arcade
Antiques centre with over 95 stallholders. Antiques and textiles in all price ranges. Good for a rummage.
26 High Street, Hungerford
Berkshire RG17 0NF
www.hungerfordarcade.co.uk

few and far – unique finds
Beautiful old and new products, furniture, clothes, tableware toys and crafts. Seasonally changing and very carefully chosen from artisans and producers around the world.
242 Brompton Road
London SW3 2BB
Tel: 020 7225 7070   www.fewandfar.net

the old cinema
Store devoted to antique, vintage and retro items.
160 Chiswick High Road
London W4 1PR
Tel: 0208 995 4166   www.theoldcinema.co.uk

pineapple ice bucket
An eclectic mix of funky things dating from the 1950s to the 1980s.
The Retro Room @ Squirrels
Lyndhurst Road, Brockenhurst
Hampshire SO42 7RL
Tel: 07753 747297   www.pineappleicebucket.co.uk

Luna
Specialists in 20th-century objects for the home.
139 Lower Parliament Street
Nottingham NG1 1EE
Tel: 0115 924 3267   www.luna-online.co.uk

frasers aerospace
Suppliers of specialist, aerospace industry-approved cleaning and maintenance products. For metal polishing.
Tel: 020 8597 8781
www.frasersaerospace.com/metalpolishing.html

KP Woodburning Stoves
Affordable and individually crafted woodburning stoves.
Tel: 07764 813867   www.kpwoodburningstove.co.uk

awning poles
Suppliers of tent and awning poles, guy ropes and accessories.
www.leisurefayre.co.uk

vintage-style awnings
Suppliers of retro-styled awnings and accessories.
www.vintagetrailersupply.com

awning, deck-chair and windbreak canvas
Supplier by the metre of vintage-style, cotton-striped canvas.
www.deckchairstripes.com

wooden windbreak poles
Suppliers of metal-tipped wooden windbreak poles.
www.outdoorworld.co.uk

auto jumble ~ beaulieu
Huge annual event. Traders selling memorabilia, parts, accessories
and vintage car caravan finds.
www.internationalautojumble.co.uk

plankbridge shepherds' huts
Manufacturers of contemporary shepherds' huts, using sustainable
and locally sourced materials.
Tel: 01305 848123   www.plankbridge.com

snail trail
Retro, beautifully restored VW campervans to rent.
Tel: 01767 600440   www.snailtrail.co.uk

airstream
Manufacturer of the icon aluminium caravan.
www.airstream.com

vintage airstream UK
Dealer and renter of vintage Airstreams.
Tel: 01684 274755 or 07766 704896   www.vintageairstreams.co.uk

vintage american caravans ltd
Importers and restorers of vintage American trailers.
Tel: 01962 773099   www.american-caravans.co.uk

tin travel trailers
Suppliers of vintage American trailers.
Tel: 001 541 891 0355 or 001 541 850 2009
www.tininntraveltrailers.com

the retro caravan company
Specialist in 1950s, 60s and 70s European caravans.
Neil Parry-Thomson
Tel: 07973 571071   www.retrocaravancompany.com

vintage trailer supply
Spare parts galore for your vintage American caravan.
www.vintagetrailersupply.com

the caravan club
Tel: 01342 326944 for general enquiries
Tel : 0800 328 6635 for membership enquiries
www.thecaravanclub.co.uk

vintage vacations
Vintage American trailers for hire on the beautiful Isle of Wight.
Tel: 07802 758113
www.vintagevacations.co.uk

la rosa campsite
An environmental approach to caravanning.
Whitby, North Yorkshire
Tel: 01947 606981   www.larosa.co.uk

sumners pond campsite
Campsite and fishery in West Sussex
Tel: 01403 732539 www.sumnerspond.co.uk

belrepayre airstream and retro trailer park
Retro-style campsite where you can bring your own caravan
or rent one.
Perry and Coline
Near Mirepoix, (09) Ariège, Midi-Pyrénées, France
www.airstreameurope.com

credits

We would like to thank all the caravan owners for allowing us to photograph their 'cool caravans'.

All photography by Hilary Walker unless otherwise stated.
www.hilarywalker.com.au

acknowledgements

Jane Field-Lewis and Chris Haddon would like to thank everyone involved for their help in putting this book together.

We have been overwhelmed with the support we have received. We would particularly like to thank all the caravan owners who so enthusiastically submitted photographs for consideration, assisted us with locations and made themselves available at sometimes short notice. Particular thanks are due to Nikki Nichol from The Caravan Club for all her contacts, help and use of the Ecostream, to Angela Cox, Caravan Club curator at the National Motor Museum, Beaulieu, Hampshire, and to Andrew Jenkinson for his knowledge and support.

Special thanks to Simon and Jenny at Sumners Pond for all their assistance in finding us locations.

Finally, thank you to our publisher Fiona Holman and our designer Georgina Hewitt at Pavilion Books for guiding us through the process.

jane field-lewis and chris haddon

Jane Field-Lewis is a London-based stylist working in film and photography. She co-owns a 1970s retro-modern styled caravan – a perfect little hideaway which inspires creativity. Chris Haddon has a passion for retro-caravanning and runs his design agency from a converted 1960s Airstream. He also owns a 1970s British and a 1970s Airstream caravan, both of which are used for short breaks with his family.

Additional captions: page 1 winchester pipet; pages 2–3 smv-10; page 4 international; page 6 frank's; page 9 winchester pipet; pages 10–11 amphibious caravan; pages 28–29 freeman; pages 44–45 monza 1000; pages 62–63 old shepherd's hut; pages 78–79 shasta; pages 100–101 safari 14/2; pages 110–111 willerby vogue; pages 120–121 airstream bambi; pages 136–137 globetrotter; page 160 land yacht

First published in 2010 by Pavilion Books
An imprint of Anova Books Company Ltd
10 Southcombe Street
London W14 0RA

www.anovabooks.com

Commissioning editor Fiona Holman
Photography by Hilary Walker
Design Steve Russell

Text copyright © Jane Field-Lewis and Chris Haddon 2010
Design copyright © Pavilion Books 2010

A CIP catalogue for this book is available from the British Library

ISBN 978-1-862-05878-1

10 9 8 7 6 5 4

Colour reproduction by Dot Gradations Ltd, UK
Printed and bound by Imago in China